HOMETOWN HUMAN

Abhijit Naskar is the twenty-first century Neuroscientist whose contributions in Cognitive and Behavioral Neuroscience have helped the world tackle the issues of systemic racism, prejudice, hate, extremism, discrimination and biases more effectively. As an untiring advocate of mental health and universal acceptance, he became a beloved best-selling author all over the world with his very first book "The Art of Neuroscience in Everything". With his pioneering ventures into the Neuropsychology of beliefs and biases, he has hugely contributed in the eradication of religious and cultural differences in our world, for which he is popularly hailed as the humanitarian scientist, who takes the human civilization in the path of sweet general harmony.

HOMETOWN
HUMAN

To Live For Soil
and Society

ABHIJIT NASKAR

Hometown Human: To Live For Soil and Society

Copyright © 2021 Abhijit Naskar

This is a work of non-fiction

All rights reserved. No part of this publication may be reproduced, distributed, or transmitted in any form or by any means, including photocopying, recording, or other electronic or mechanical methods, without the prior written permission of the author, except in the case of brief quotations embodied in critical reviews and certain other noncommercial uses permitted by copyright law.

An Amazon Publishing Company, 1st Edition, 2021

Printed in the United States of America

ISBN: 9798525040779

Also by Abhijit Naskar

The Art of Neuroscience in Everything
Your Own Neuron: A Tour of Your Psychic Brain
The God Parasite: Revelation of Neuroscience
The Spirituality Engine
Love Sutra: The Neuroscientific Manual of Love
Homo: A Brief History of Consciousness
Neurosutra: The Abhijit Naskar Collection
Autobiography of God: Biopsy of A Cognitive Reality
Biopsy of Religions: Neuroanalysis towards Universal
Tolerance
Prescription: Treating India's Soul
What is Mind?
In Search of Divinity: Journey to The Kingdom of Conscience
Love, God & Neurons: Memoir of a scientist who found
himself by getting lost
The Islamophobic Civilization: Voyage of Acceptance
Neurons of Jesus: Mind of A Teacher, Spouse & Thinker
Neurons, Oxygen & Nanak
The Education Decree
Principia Humanitas
The Krishna Cancer
Rowdy Buddha: The First Sapiens
We Are All Black: A Treatise on Racism
The Bengal Tigress: A Treatise on Gender Equality
Either Civilized or Phobic: A Treatise on Homosexuality
Wise Mating: A Treatise on Monogamy
Illusion of Religion: A Treatise on Religious
Fundamentalism
The Film Testament
Human Making is Our Mission: A Treatise on Parenting
I Am The Thread: My Mission
7 Billion Gods: Humans Above All
Lord is My Sheep: Gospel of Human
Morality Absolute
A Push in Perception
Let The Poor Be Your God
Conscience over Nonsense
Saint of The Sapiens
Time to Save Medicine
Fabric of Humanity
Build Bridges not Walls: In the name of Americana
The Constitution of The United Peoples of Earth

Lives to Serve Before I Sleep
When Humans Unite: Making A World Without Borders
All For Acceptance
Monk Meets World
Mission Reality
Citizens of Peace: Beyond The Savagery of Sovereignty
Operation Justice: To Make A Society That Needs No Law
See No Gender
The Gospel of Technology
Every Generation Needs Caretakers: The Gospel of
Patriotism
Aşkanjali: The Sufi Sermon
Mad About Humans: World Maker's Almanac
Revolution Indomable
When Call The People: My World My Responsibility
No Foreigner Only Family
Hurricane Humans: Give me accountability, I'll give you
peace
Ain't Enough to Look Human
Servitude is Sanctitude
Time To End Democracy: The Meritocratic Manifesto
I Vicdansaadet Speaking: No Rest Till The World is Lifted
Boldly Comes Justice: Sentient not Silent
Good Scientist: When Science and Service Combine
Sleepless for Society
Neden Türk: The Gospel of Secularism
Martyr Meets World: To Solve The Hard Problem of
Inhumanity
The Shape of A Human: Our America Their America
When Veins Ignite: Either Integration or Degradation
Heart Force One: Need No Gun to Defend Society
Solo Standing on Guard: Life Before Law
Generation Corazon: Nationalism is Terrorism
Mucize Insan: When The World is Family

DEDICATION

*This book is dedicated to all the
Naskareans on Discord.*

CONTENTS

1.   No Such Thing As Activism

Hurt me I'll spare, hurt people I'll devour. Thus speaks a human being - someone who is an ordinary person but has an extraordinary character - someone who is not famous, but has an actual, genuine responsibleness for the society, unlike most of the famous celebrities who have everything in life so the only way they can draw more attention is by pretending to be a humanitarian or an activist.

You see, almost every celebrity - every single famous personality, calls themselves an activist. You know why? Because, the term activist no longer means anything, it's just yet another fashion trend, something that makes you look cool and hip. To them I say, you are not the model human to talk about the fundamental rights of humankind, while standing next to your million dollar supercar, for you are part of the problem - you are part of the paradigm that facilitates and sustains disparity.

First, learn to live a simple life, regardless of whether you are famous or not, then talk about social justice. It is this simple, until all of us have abundance, none of us is entitled to abundance. But the fact of the matter is, a fraction of the human population have all the abundance because of the lack of fundamentals among the rest of humanity. And standing up on the conviction of equal distribution of resources is not activism, it's just plain humanity.

Know this - a real activist, someone who gives their life to improve the society, never calls themselves an activist or humanitarian, just like a person who is really above the prejudices of the past, never calls themselves woke. Wokeness and activism are mere fashion trends, nothing more. And only those with substance in their character will feel this simple fact, rest will only rebel against it, just like they rebel against everything else in society, because to them misbehavior is a declaration of independence.

Let me tell you this, we didn't trudge through 3.5 billion years of evolution, so that we could carry on with the same freaking acts of recklessness and selfishness as we used to in the jungle. Civilization cannot exist without responsibility, and yes, that indeed requires unorthodoxy, but it ought to be an accountable unorthodoxy.

This recklessness of the seemingly civilized population is one of the reasons why greedy corporations and control-freak governments are able to work their tactics of occupation in various corner of the world.

But here's the thing, occupation has no place in civilized society. Wherever there is occupation of any sort, be it economic occupation through capitalist exploitation or occupation of land in the name of sovereignty, there is human rights violation, and wherever there is a violation of the fundamental rights of people, nothing civilized can flourish there.

And as such, it is imperative that occupation, imperialism and colonialism of any kind are abolished from every corner of the world. For example, it is time, Palestine redeemed freedom from Israeli occupation, Scotland from British occupation, and Jammu and Kashmir from Indian occupation. If you ask why – I say this – it's because, until all of us are free, none of us is free.

6

2.   **Sonnet of Phony Activism**

Sonnet of Phony Activism

Those who give their life to society,
Never call themselves activist.
Those who work night and day for others,
Rarely identify as reformist.
It's only the vane, lame and the shallow,
Who draw attention with phony activism.
Those who actually care for society,
Live a life of sacrifice beyond definition.
Activist and woke are actually code,
That says, look at me I am so great.
Real greats don't care about labels,
They're martyred for others without regret.
The world doesn't need more phony label.
What's needed is humans being accountable.

3. Sonnet of Occupation

Sonnet of Occupation

With just weeks of lockdown,
You all feel restless and bland.
That is how everyday life is,
For people in occupied land.
Imagine living your whole life,
Subject to restriction and suspicion.
Ask a Palestinian or a Kashmiri,
They'll reveal the face of occupation.
Life, liberty and happiness,
Are the rights of every being.
Whenever a government violates them,
Civilized humanity must intervene.
I call to all humans far and near,
Rest not till statehood is declared.

4. While The Able Are Busy Boozing

16

If you want to find out whether the people of a country are unfree- whether they are living under oppression, don't listen to the state, look at the conditions of the people. Whether in the name of diplomacy or just for the sake of saving the face of the nation, the state can rarely walk along the line of truth.

Thus a government can commit even acts of terrorism in the name of national security, yet not be held accountable as a terrorist organization is held accountable. Acts of terror committed by a government is still terrorism. But mark you, do not confuse the acts of a government with religion. Let's take the atrocities of Israeli government for example. You cannot judge 15 millions Jews of the world, based on the actions of one terrorist organization, called the Israeli government. Government may use religion as a means of controlling people, like the backward-heading state of Turkey is doing right now, but they must never be considered synonymous.

Now comes the question – how on earth can these barbaric atrocities continue in a so-called civilized society? And the answer is - all of this inhumanity is possible because those who are actually capable of moving mountains if they want, are busy rebelling against the norms of society by wearing ripped jeans or smoking weed. To them I say, enough with this childishness – grow up already - lives are at stake here! You have the power to move mountains, yet all you are excited about is getting high and getting laid!

Grow up and bring all that enthusiasm, all that boldness, all that bravery to some real civilized use. Grow up and become an actual living revolution against the real atrocities committed on millions and millions of innocent people across the world on a daily basis. Wanna do some rebellion? Get your priorities straight. First learn to distinguish between an act of revolution that betters the society and a childish act of rebellion that only butters your shallow vanity.

Let me put it to you straight. You wanna try booze, try it - you wanna try weed, try it – you wanna get laid, go get laid - just do it all and get it over with, so that you can pay attention to the real troubles of society. How dare you waste your life on nonsense! You may say, it is your life, and you can do whatever you want with it. To that I say, it is not your life, it is human life, and a human life that doesn't come to the aid of the society is anything but human. So, as long as you consider yourself human, you have a responsibility towards society - towards society mark you, not to social norms.

5.   Obeying Norms is Not Accountability

Social norms have no bearing over social responsibility, in fact, given the current developmental state of the social psyche, obeying the norms of society would require a conscientious person to act as the most irresponsible and uncivilized creature on earth. So you see, obeying the norms of society has nothing to do with you being a responsible human of society.

Standing up to the uncivilized norms is one thing and disobeying norms just to prove that you are above the norms is another. The former leads the society in a civilized direction whereas the latter leads the society down the path of degradation and uncivilization.

Let me put this into perspective. Those who disobey all norms just for the sake of defiance, do so to feel different from and superior to everyone else, whereas those who stand up to the uncivilized norms, do so not to belittle anyone, but to lift everyone up. Here's the thing - misdemeanor and recklessness are no more civilized than prejudice and superstition.

Change requires character, and where there is character, courage comes on its own. And recklessness is no sign of character, if anything, it is the most primitive form of savagery. You don't need to wear a fancy uniform to better the society, you just need to act out of responsibility, instead of reckless and disobedience.

Be restless in concern, not reckless in disobedience. Remember, a life without people is worse than death, so defying people accomplishes nothing - because you may defy the whole world in a shallow attempt to prove that you are different, but in the end, you'll be more miserable than ever, because you've foolishly distanced yourself from the world.

6. To Give is To Live

In a world that applauds selfishness, if you are unselfish, then you are indeed different, and you no longer need to pretend to be different. So, be you, not for being different, but because you can't be anything else. The sun's contribution to the world is incomparable to any other celestial body, yet the sun never tries to be different, it just keeps on giving all the light that life on earth needs, not because it is superior, but because for the sun to give is to live.

It is that unruffled, untainted desire to give that makes a human out of an animal. It is this simple, to take is animal, to give is human. You see, all of us are born animal, it's with our acts of unselfishness and self-correction that we become human - that we become civilized. But mark you, mending our errors to become civilized is not woke, it's human, just like drinking water to stay alive is not woke, it's life.

Let me give you an example. And for that let's take our beloved America - our beloved land of liberty. No matter how much we take pride in the history of America, the fact of the matter is, the nation called America was founded not upon the pillars of principles but of atrocities. And, it'll take a lifetime for at least the next ten generations of Americans to make amends for the wrongs done throughout the bigoted history of America.

But here's the thing. There's not a single nation on earth whose history is not replete with inhumanity. And that's because inhumanity was the default mode of action during the time of our ancestors. However, turning a blind eye to them won't solve anything either. What we can do, is acknowledge them and take the conscious and determined pledge to never let them be repeated. And this involves self-correction.

7.   Sonnet of Nazi America

30

Sonnet of Nazi America

America is the land of liberty,
Offer available only to white people.
When it comes to people of color,
It's a Nazi nation though unofficial.
If you are white and you make a mistake,
You are most likely to receive a warning.
But if you are a person of color or muslim,
Better have a good reason for breathing.
They say we live in a democratic land,
A system of, by and for the people.
But what they forget to teach in school,
People doesn't really mean every individual.
No one can change the past that's for sure.
Defying all supremacy we must rise and roar.

8.   **Sonnet of National Beauty**

Sonnet of National Beauty

Beauty and ugliness as we know them,
Are the product of an ugly mind.
Once we step across all pretenses,
We learn how much we've been blind.
The whitest places on planet earth,
Happen to be the ugliest of all places.
For what appears to be a fancy joint,
Is filled with a bunch of suited savages.
Nations of color have problems too,
But they don't pretend to be advanced.
When we claim to be a global leader,
We must first practice inclusion on demand.
Great is not the nation that appears fancy,
But one which values people over diplomacy.

9. Out of The Woods of Biases

The road to a civilized world goes through the dark woods of biases. Now let me be clear on something. Every animal is born in these woods, including us humans - none of us is born outside of it, no matter how much some people delude themselves with the comforting notion that they have no biases to begin with.

If you can conquer your biases, then only can you see the light of civilization, nay, then only can you be the light of civilization. Civilization lies nowhere else, but inside of us. But it is dormant. To awaken that civilization you must first conquer your animal nature. And this conquest is not a one-time endeavor, it is life itself. And this conquest is rarely going to be easy, in fact, often you are going to be confronted with unforeseeable circumstances. Let me give you an example.

We are finally beginning to recognize that there's more to gender than just male and female. And now that we have recognized it, we are taking baby steps in the path of integration. And that brings its own unforeseeable mistakes - mistakes that are easily amendable. Take the world of sports for instance.

Some may feel super woke to say that transgender women athletes belong in female sports, but let me tell you as a biologist, in terms of muscle mass, transgender women have similar advantages over females as male athletes do, even with testosterone suppression therapy, therefore, it is not enough to simply acknowledge transgender as a distinct gender, we must also make necessary alterations to our preexisting societal fields, such as setting up transgender category in sports, where performance is predicated on physiological attributes, so that in an attempt to vest upon the transgender population their long-overdue fundamental rights, we do not start treating other genders unfairly without even being aware of it.

This is another kind of implicit bias, quite similar to the blindness of the racist towards their innate racism, so it must be treated as we treat any other implicit bias in society that causes harm. Gender has no bearing on a person's character and mental faculties, but it does have a fundamental bearing on a person's physiological features and capacities.

You see, I don't care about sports, that is, I don't have any particular affinity towards it. The only sport I've ever engaged in is martial arts. But so long as a sport is categorized based on gender, it is only civilized to come up with a new category when there's a previously unaccepted, hence new gender. It is this simple, we cannot fit a multi-gender world into a two-gender system of sports. It is not resistance to transgender athletes, it is called evolution of sports in accordance with the evolution of society.

Remember, replacing one wrong with another is not rightness. Our purpose is to preserve the rights of everyone, not to change the shape of the violation of those rights. Building a civilized society without any human rights violation takes time, but so long as the human psyche within the human body is willing to correct its errors, nothing can stop us from achieving it.

10. Wokeness is No Measure

44

Wokeness is no measure of civilization, just like traditions are no measure of civilization. Even wokeness can deceive you, just like traditions have been deceiving humankind for ages. So, place your attention on becoming civilized, not on adjusting to the label of woke. All labels are a step down from human, hence must be scrutinized closely.

There is not a single label concocted by the puny mind of human that can match the character of a human. You know why, because the title human itself is the purest force of evolution, rest are lesser replicas. That is why even the title Neuroscientist fails to define who I am. It may give you a general idea about my work, but it says absolutely nothing about my character, just like titles such as preacher, teacher, janitor, american, mexican, british and so on are capable of saying nothing about the character of a person. Only the title Human can do that, if and only if, a creature wholeheartedly accepts that title above all other empty labels along with the responsibility that goes along with it.

I am using the term creature on purpose, because that's what all of us are, unless we accept the responsibility of being human. As I've said in my previous works, the title Human is not some family heirloom that you inherit by birth - you have to earn it with your own actions. Conquer your animal nature first, then call yourself human.

11. Freedom Alone Won't Do

If every corner of the world had a handful of humans who have conquered their animal nature, there wouldn't be any need for law. This may sound like a utopian notion but it is not at all impossible. But let's assume that the world will continue to need law for a long time - even then, it is imperative for the residents of earth to conquer their animal nature, for that is the whole point of being a civilized lifeform.

Always say to yourself - my world, my responsibility. Responsibility is born of love. If you love this world, you'd want to grow on your own. This is the problem with the population, everybody wants all the freedom in the world, but none of the responsibility that goes along with it. And such a society is no more advanced than a bunch of cave people.

This is the reason why people are going crazy over cryptocurrency. All they see is the decentralization part and they think, since nobody is in control of the whole thing, it must be something revolutionary. It's like saying, life in the wild is so liberating, it must be revolutionary.

You see, in practice, control is another name for regulation and responsibility, which is what the masses hate. And that's how callous and shallow civilians of planet earth want the society to be - all the freedom and none of the accountability. But I beg to say to these backboneless beasts, there is no civilization without accountability.

Let me put this in perspective. Cryptocurrency would be a great boon to society, if used within the centralized framework of the current financial system, but if used in a decentralized fashion, it'd only facilitate disparity and instability.

The belief that technology will solve every single problem of society, is what I call digital fundamentalism, which is as dangerous as religious fundamentalism. You think cryptocurrency will solve all the economic disparities in the world - it won't, because the traditional centralized financial system is not the problem, the problem is greed and indifference. So long as there is greed in the society, every innovation in such society will end up causing more disparities rather than solving them.

12. Sonnet of Cryptocurrency

52

Sonnet of Cryptocurrency

The reason people are nuts about cryptocurrency,
Is that they hear the magic phrase regulation-free.
But what they forget to take into account,
Is that it also means the user alone bears liability.
The purpose behind a centralized system,
Is not exploitation but to provide trust and stability.
Anything that is decentralized on the other hand,
Is a breeding ground for fraud and volatility.
Not every fancy innovation is gonna benefit society,
Innovation without accountability is only delusion.
Cryptocurrency can be a great boon to banking,
If it merges with the centralized financial institution.
Intoxication of tech is yet another fundamentalism.
Algorithm without humanity is digital barbarism.

13. When The People Are Shallow

Forget the corrupt politicians and billionaires, get hold of your own greed first. Learn to distinguish between necessity and luxury. Why do you think Apple can become the first trillion dollar company in history, not because they can innovate, but because they can abuse the shallowness and vanity of the masses.

It is the people that place institutions on a pedestal, if the people were truly responsible and conscientious, there wouldn't be any institution on any pedestal - heck, there wouldn't even be any pedestal, for each individual would know their role in society and they would carry out that role with utmost responsibility without giving in to vanity and superstition. In such a society, there wouldn't be any need for reformers, for each human would be a reformer themselves.

Politicians come and politicians go, but reformers are eternal. And who is the reformer? Each and every human who is accountable for their society is the reformer. Indifference and callousness have no place in the life of such human. In fact, indifference and callousness have no role in any human life, yet indifference and callousness run through the very veins of the masses, then they shout, 'it's the fault of the politicians, it's the fault of the billionaires, it's the fault of the doctors, it's the fault of the scientists, it's the fault of the teachers.' What a hypocrisy! What a waste!

14. Sonnet of Luxury

Sonnet of Luxury

Serenity shrinks as luxury grows,
While you pay moderation no heed.
Disparity is not a matter of economics,
All of it is born of human greed.
Moderation is the key to contentment,
Lesser the needs the happier you are.
Grow up and get hold of your needs,
Learn to tell necessities from desire.
Cherish the little things in life,
Value people over possession.
A healthy society is born of healthy mind,
Health begins where ends self-obsession.
Sophistication is an enemy of life.
A life of simplicity is bound to thrive.

15. Power To People Doesn't Mean Power

64

Be responsible and all will be well with society, if not, then all the cryptocurrencies in the world won't be able to fix our society. You see, there is more to the phrase "power to people", than mere liberty. "Power to people" doesn't mean power, it means responsibility, that is, it has very little to do with power and way more to do with accountability. And that part about accountability somehow remains absent from all the narratives on civics and democracy.

Adult babies have a tendency to believe that a society without any regulatory institution of any sort is somehow a better society, but it's not, because until those babies grow up and learn to take responsibility for themselves, absence of regulation will cause only more disparities and degradation. Imagine a world where the private individual is able to do absolutely anything they want, without being held accountable for their actions – in such a world, though a handful of individuals will remain accountable with or without regulations, the vast majority of the population will destroy themselves in a matter of weeks.

There's no such thing as activism, there's only accountability. Either you are accountable, or you ain't human. And I wish I could tell you that people will act accountable even without the presence of regulation or law of any kind, but the hard reality of the matter is, they won't, not in our present developmental stage as a childish, foolish and self-obsessed lifeform. Hence, till the people become accountable themselves, we must enforce accountability by superficial means, such as regulations, policy and law.

And considering the neurological tenets of the human brain, if they continue to pretend to be accountable and act on that accountability, in time, may be not soon, but in a distant future, recklessness is bound to become an alien concept to the human species. In simple terms, today we enforce accountability, so that our future generation can act accountable out of their own free will without the support from superficial regulatory institutions.

16. I Dream of A World Civilized
(The Sonnet)

I Dream of A World Civilized
(The Sonnet)

I dream of a world civilized,
Where color of skin is nothing.
But when I look at the present,
It poses a challenge to my dreaming.
I envision a society night and day,
Where law is not necessary.
But when I look at the world today,
I realize how far it's from reality.
I dream of a world most human,
Beyond all gender and sexuality.
But when I look at the moment's truth,
It is far too distant from that humanity.
Yet difficulties only add value to a dream.
If not today when will our journey begin!

17. The Greatest Force of Reform

Law may be a superficial means to enforce accountability, as I've pointed out in my previous works, but it is the second most effective means we have so far. You may be wondering, what is the most effective means to instill accountability, and the answer is, education, but not the kind of education that produces mechanical slaves, rather the kind of education that strengthens the mind's natural curiosity while nourishing their character as a whole human being - a human being who thinks of the benefit of others before thinking of their own - a human being who cares less about receiving and more about giving, about helping.

You see, there's no healer, only helper. And with the right kind of education, every child turns into an active helper of society, hence, a living, breathing, whole human being. And that's what a truly accountable human society looks like, where the individuals act human out of their own free will, not because they are obligated to do so under law.

So, to put it simply, education is the greatest force of social reform, but for education to reform society, we must reform education first. And if this reform in education doesn't rise out of the parents' and teachers' own initiative, there again comes the need for regulations or law. For example, if a school is unwilling to include black history in their school curriculum, it is the civilized duty of the state to make that school legally bound to include black history, because when we talk about the history of America, Black history is American history.

In fact, just for the sake of understanding, and not to prove superiority or inferiority of any one community over the other, if we measure the amount of blood and sweat that actually went into the making of America, we'd find that the contributions of the blacks far outweigh the contributions of the whites!

But that's not the point. The point is, white supremacy is not a human right, it's a human rights violation, and by allowing a school to keep black history out of their curriculum, a government only perpetuates white supremacy, hence it perpetuates a human rights violation, and what's the point of having a government that doesn't have the guts to stand up to a human rights violation! Is this why we broke our backs trying to bring down the Trump administration!

In fact, advocacy of supremacy of any kind of sect is a violation of human rights. With the sense of supremacy comes the sense of perfection, and with the sense of perfection comes the deterioration of society. Hence, supremacy is injurious to the health and development of society, whereas self-correction is fundamental for the health and development of society.

18. The Juneteenth Sonnet

The Juneteenth Sonnet

Once upon a time but not long ago,
They brought us to America in chains.
Thinking of themselves as superior race,
White barbarians kept us as slaves.
But the sapling of humanity found a way,
To break those chains causing ascension.
Whites and blacks all stood up together,
And lighted the torch of emancipation.
Juneteenth is now declared holiday,
Yet to some it feels like a critical dishonor.
The human race comes from a black mother,
Yet they treat people of color as inferior.
The America handed to us is far from civilized.
But together we'll make our home humanized.

19. Sonnet of National Obligation

82

Sonnet of National Obligation

When a nation is founded on terrorism,
It has an obligation for self-improvement.
If admitting the past hurts your feelings,
Better remain in your mother's basement.
If we really look for filth and atrocities,
We'll find it in the history of every nation.
The real problem is not the history,
But the absolute denial of its admission.
No nation can become civilized,
Till it steps up to right the wrongs.
Admit the errors of our ancestors,
And pledge to never repeat those harms.
Humanity begins with admitting inhumanity.
Lo we are the shield against further atrocity.

20. Growth is Life

Self-proclaimed supremacy has plagued humankind since time immemorial. And abolition of such prehistoric behavior is a fundamental requirement of civilization. What this means in practical life is that you are mindful of your shortcomings as well as your strongholds and you work ceaselessly to strengthen your strongholds while eliminating your shortcomings. You try neither to boast about your strongholds nor to cover up your shortcomings. You just live as a whole human being who grows constantly without ever showing any resistance to self-correction.

Question yourself, question the world, question everything that comes along your way, for as I've said before, once you start to question, you'll start to learn. And remember, the question of why behind every phenomenon in nature, does not have one answer, it has infinite layers of answer, and the more layers you unravel, the closer you get to understanding the makeup of the universe. So question, and you shall understand – yourself, the society and the universe – basically, it all starts with the capacity to question.

Question leads to correction and correction leads to growth, hence correction, that is, self-correction is fundamental for life, because growth is life. Hence, denial of one's flaws is against life itself. Thus, flawlessness has no place in a civilized society. We can grow only when we accept that we are flawed by default - all of us. And this applies not just to the individual, but to all aspects of society. Let's take law for example.

We can never make a flawless system of law, because to assume any system to be flawless is to assume that it is above scrutiny, and any system that is assumed to be above scrutiny ends up doing more harm to the society than good, hence what you call loopholes, I call the strongpoints of law that allow for the will of the people to have the final say, no matter how invincible those in power feel themselves to be.

From time to time, these loopholes may be abused by the greedy buffoons, but they are fundamental to facilitate a functional democracy. Therefore, perfection should never be our aim in any field of society - our aim must always be ceaseless self-correction. The moment we assume something to be perfection, we lose all desire for improvement, and the moment we lose the desire for improvement, we lose all possibility of growth.

21. Never Aim For Perfection

Imperfection facilitates improvement, perfection facilitates stagnation. Therefore, never aim for perfection - perfection is anti-life. Aim for evolution, aim for growth, aim for ceaseless improvement. For example, there was a time when state and church were one entity. But eventually humankind realized that decrees and doctrines written by dead people based on not facts, evidence or reason, but plain whim, do not make good foundation for a civilized society, hence, we severed the state from the church, that is, religion.

However, this hasn't stopped religious bigotry and boneheadedness from infecting the society or the state. The heartbeat bill of Texas is one such example, which violates human rights by making abortion illegal. But here's the thing, until the state or the church takes full responsibility for a newborn without claiming custody, no bill or bible is qualified to even offer suggestions on a woman's right to abortion.

You see, nature has made it ridiculously easy to make babies - it's no miracle. It takes a few seconds and no skill whatsoever to make a baby - heck, it takes more effort to produce pizza than offspring. So making a baby is no big deal, you are not achieving something extraordinary, you are just doing what every animal does, but what's important is to raise a baby in a stable environment. And if one is not able to provide any stability to their child, the only civilized alternative is to abort.

The point is, when someone assumes a two-thousand year old book to be perfection, there is no reasoning with such a person. Counting this book of mine that you are reading, I have written seventy books, but I am super delighted to state that I cannot call any of them perfection, for all of them could be improved, if I had to rewrite them. And that's precisely where the beauty of life lies, in our capacity for improvement. We all have the capacity to improve ourselves, but the question is, do we want to improve?

22. Sonnet of Abortion

96

Sonnet of Abortion

My body, my decision,
Whether I choose birth or abortion.
Till a state can care for the newborn,
No bill is qualified to offer resolution.
Instead of controlling my birth canal,
Work on carving a paradigm of equality.
Build a world where a newborn is a gift,
Not a burden on life, dream or economy.
Abolish all disparities born of greed,
Strip the wealthy of their ill-gotten riches.
Use all resources for collective welfare,
So that status ends up on history pages.
Worse than aborting is birthing in instability.
I'll give birth when I need not rely on pity.

23. To Be Less Animal

So you see, we are far from civilized. The battle between civilization and uncivilization is still on, right within the fabric of our society, and it'll continue so long as humankind lives. People may look civilized on the outside, but outside appearance means nothing. For example, suits don't make people civilized, if they did, US Capitol would be the most civilized place on earth. Like the whole damned world, the US Capitol is also a mishmash of civilization and uncivilization.

It is not clothes that make us civilized, it is our willingness to improve ourselves - from tribal fiends to human beings. Human brain is fundamentally racist, for every brain is born with tribalism embedded in them meant for self-preservation. It takes a lot of resolve and ceaseless, civilized self-correction to break free from that tribalism.

There is no place for perfection in a civilized society, for anything that claims perfection, ends up claiming supremacy. That is why, we may accept a falsity that doesn't claim perfection, but we must never accept anything that claims perfection, not even a truth. You see, truth never claims to be perfect, for truth never is perfect, it is ever-evolving, it is ever-growing - that's what makes truth beautiful – truth is not static, truth is dynamic.

There is no perfection, there is only degrees of imperfection. As a matter of fact, at our current 21st century evolutionary stage we can even say that, there's no humanity, there's only degrees of animality. So to put it another way, we are not going to be human for a long time, all we can work to be is less animal. Don't try to be the best human in the world, try to be the least animal in the world, and you'd automatically be the best human in the world.

24. Supremacy is Sickness

When we use the term human to refer to a person, we are merely referring to physiological attributes not to attributes of character, and the irony of the matter is that without character no human is a human, but only a good-looking animal. On top of that, people have a tendency to consider those who look and live like themselves as more human than others. Thus racism is sustained, thus nationalism is sustained, thus all sorts of bigotry and sectarianism are sustained - all on the foundation of the 'us versus them' mentality - and that too under the banner of 'humanity'.

I'll say it to you in simple terms, sectarianism and humanity are anti-thesis of each other. But you cannot possibly convince those practicing sectarianism, of this simple yet fundamental fact of human life. You see, bigotry knows no reason, if it did, there wouldn't be any bigotry in the world. And by arguing with bigots you only infuriate and empower them. So, call them out whenever their actions are against humanity's best interest, but not as adults, rather as kid bullies.

They are not necessarily bad people, they are just mentally underdeveloped, hence they hold on to the primitive ideas of racial supremacy, cultural supremacy or religious supremacy. And though beliefs and behavior of racial, cultural and religious supremacy may not be considered clinical illness today, soon in the near future they will be considered as such.

However, I do avoid argumentation with bigots, not because I'm afraid of them, but because I'm terrified of my own anger. You see, the calmest person on earth is the most dangerous person on earth. So, to the bigots I say, do not even dare to test my patience, your existence may depend on it. I conquered myself, then only I set out to conquer the world. And how do you conquer a world - by wiping out all trace of self and placing your life at the feet of the helpless.

25. Breathing While Black
(The Sonnet)

Breathing While Black
(The Sonnet)

White folks think before going to work,
Hope I don't run into traffic on the way.
Black folks think before going to work,
Hope I don't get shot and make it safe.
White folks think before going to jog,
Hope the park is not much crowded.
Black folks think before going to jog,
Hope I don't run into someone bigoted.
White folks teach their kids before school,
Don't you dare talk to strangers.
Black folks beg their kids on knees,
Don't act smart when approached by coppers.
Whites can dream of being big and creative.
All we blacks can dream of is being able to live.

26. What is Anxiety

Real lasting happiness comes only through unselfishness, for selfishness only breeds anxiety. You see, there is no such thing as anxiety, for anxiety is alertness in action - alertness that is produced by your brain to ensure self-preservation. But if you wipe out the self from its very roots and fill every pore of your body and mind with a sense of genuine care for others, then that so-called anxiety will fade away on its own.

In short, anxiety is a product of selfishness, the more selfish you are, the more anxious you become. Be unselfish and there'll be serenity. And a consumerist culture is a perfect breeding ground for anxiety, for it feeds a person's self-absorption. In fact, professions of psychiatry, therapy and mindfulness are bound to boom in parallel with unmoderated consumerism, for unmoderated consumerism facilitates self-absorption which in turn breeds anxiety, and the more anxious you are, the more you need expert help to deal with that anxiety.

The simple and free way to be liberated from anxiety is to be unselfish, and it not only makes you healthy and content, it also transforms the society around you into a practical, tangible, real kingdom of heaven. It is this simple, the more things you buy, the more miserable you become, the more you give, the happier you'll be. You don't need to give up everything, mark you, but learn to distinguish between the things that you really need and the things that you wish to have.

Things don't make you happy, giving up the things for the benefit of the people does. Take the I, cross it out in the middle, and you have a living christ - you yourself. Oust the self from every corner of existence and turn each of those corners into an altar for society.

27. Unselfish Sonnet

Unselfish Sonnet

Unself your soul,
And lo the joy pours.
Wipe out the I,
And the world is yours.
The more selfish you are,
The more anxious you'll be.
One who's lost in service,
Is the epitome of humanity.
In a world of self-obsession,
Be the spark most selfless.
Burn yourself to ashes,
Let all bathe in your kindness.
To give is to live o human.
To die for others is salvation.

28. Instrument of Service

Turn your life into an instrument of service and you'll have all the joy in the world. Service is the purest form of love, and as I've said in one of my previous works, life is either an instrument of love or nothing at all.

So, the decision is up to you - are you going to live your life as an instrument of love, or waste it by being the instrument of selfishness, that is, savagery! Remember, the future of humanity depends on your decision. In fact, your decision is not just your decision, it is the decision of the whole humankind, for all reform starts with one person. And you don't need to be a so-called intellectual to be that person, you just need to be accountable.

Common sense and accountability are enough to revolutionize the world. You see, intelligence is only a small part of the whole picture. If intelligence could build a better world, we would already be living in a better world by the grace of all the intelligent machines that we have built. But do we?

Intelligence is a boon, but only when guided by warmth, that is love. Love above faith, love above culture, love above intellect, love above every single concoction of the human mind. Some might say, isn't love also a concoction of the mind? To which I say, it depends on your perception of love.

In this so-called modern society, what we have is not love, but corporate love, where you love another person, the same way you love your smartphone, you love because you receive a sense of pleasure from them. And this so-called love is not some fancy new concoction of the mind, it is a savage survival drive vested in us by nature.

The love I am talking about is the kind of love that gives all and expects nothing in return, the kind of love that is pure and chaste, devoid of all selfishness. And this love is indeed to be produced by the human mind - human mind, mark you, not something that looks like a human, but behaves like a savage. Only with such pure, incorruptible, expectationless and timeless love born of the true human mind can we build a true human civilization.

29. Leap Beyond Libido
(The Sonnet)

124

Leap Beyond Libido
(The Sonnet)

Brotherhood won't do,
Nor will sisterhood.
What the world really needs,
Is a sense of humanhood.
So long as gender lingers,
In the behavior of human.
We'll not have a society,
Free from sexualization.
Genitalia have no role in society,
Other than in bed.
When you leap beyond libido,
Even a naked body seems sacred.
The body has evolved to crave for release,
But a well-built character is hard to please.

30. Sonnet of Breastfeeding

Sonnet of Breastfeeding

From the breasts a world is fed,
With their warmth society is raised.
Yet we ignore their sacred place,
Without breasts we'll all be erased.
Woman's breasts are not objects,
With or without a baby clinging.
We may hail them means of pleasure,
Only when the person is asking.
Way more than triggers of romance,
Breasts are symbolic of motherhood.
A society that doesn't respect mothers,
Will never ever attain humanhood.
A world that is safe for mothers,
Is safe for all beyond age and genders.

31. No Such Thing As Philanthropy

What does the animal salesman know about the universe of love! Animals cannot enter that universe, only those who have cleansed themselves of all selfishness will experience that ever-effulgent universe. You know why – because the ever-effulgent, revolutionary universe of love is born of the unselfish heart. It doesn't exist anywhere outside - it doesn't exist up there in the sky, in some extraterrestrial plane - it's all inside of you.

So, want to have a righteous and just world – become love yourself first, by unselfing your soul. And by being unselfish, I don't mean the phony unselfishness of the so-called philanthropists. Let me elaborate why. You see, there is no such thing as philanthropy, because the money that the billionaires pretend to donate, belong to the people anyways. So what this world really needs is for the people to compel the governments to enforce wealth tax on the super rich, so that the ridiculous disparities in our economic structure do not occur in the first place.

And this can happen only when the citizens have a backbone with a genuine desire for growth - citizens constantly chasing luxury won't do, for citizens chasing luxury are the very cause of the economic disparities of the world, not the billionaires. Serenity shrinks where luxury grows.

And here's the thing, we may pursue comfort to some extent, but never luxury, for luxury is injurious to growth. And then too, nobody has a right to comfort, unless everybody has access to the essentials of life. And this simple principle of civilized existence cannot be realized by the self-absorbed, megalomaniacal, boneheaded, prehistoric savage.

32. Individuals Over Institutions

If your desire for equality overwhelms your primeval drive for self-absorption, then and then alone will there be hope for real upliftment, rights and justice in the human society. An everyday, ordinary, unbending desire for the good of everyone, that's what'll save humanity from its imminent, self-imposed doom, not some fancy United Nations assemblies, and some soup kitchens.

Make it a habit to feed at least one hungry person in your neighborhood every day, and there won't be any need for soup-kitchens in the world. Just people taking care of people - that's the simple gospel for a happy, healthy and prosperous living. There may come a thousand United Nations and a thousand humanitarian organizations, my hopes are still pinned on the actions of the individual. It's the individuals who'll save the world, not institutions.

Here some may say, building organizations is a way for individuals to come together and become stronger as a collective. And that is completely fine. I am not against them - more power to them! But what I want you the individual to realize is that you already belong to one big, natural organization, it's called humanity. So remember this, when individuals stand up, institutions collapse.

I place all my hopes upon you, o courageous being of conscience and character - you the individual - if not the world, take a portion of this world upon your shoulders and lift it up into the light of illumination. Once the citizens take responsibility, politicians will lose their job. This is not socialism, it's just plain humanity.

Some people call me a socialist, to which I say, what is socialism if not an ordinary sense of responsibility towards society! And here, the term socialism is of no consequence, what matters is the responsibility towards society. You may call yourself socialist, you may not - it is of no significance, what really matters is, do you feel responsible for the welfare of society!

33. Come Down To The Soil of Humanity

The world doesn't need socialism, it doesn't need communism, it doesn't even need humanism, all it needs is for the humans to act human. This action may be defined by different people differently, but those labels are of no consequence. The definition is not the act. But the point is, people of intellect cannot fathom this, nor can the people of rituals, only beings of love will realize this simple fact of life in their bones.

You see, intellect may give you knowledge, but it doesn't make you a decent human being. Let me elaborate with a few examples. An intellectual standpoint is not necessarily a human standpoint. From an intellectual standpoint you may say all lives matter, but when you come down to the ground of humanity, then you realize the inhuman atrocities that people of color face on a daily basis, as opposed to the white people – then you realize the wide range of suspicions people of color face just because they look darker than the whites.

From an intellectual standpoint you may say Juneteenth is meaningless, for there is only one independence day, it's July fourth, but when you come down to the ground of humanity, then you realize what a simple act such as a nationwide acknowledgement of historical wrongs committed on an entire community of people means to that particular community emotionally.

When you come down to the ground of humanity from your pedestal of intellect, then you realize that though white Americans received independence from British occupation on July 4th, 1776, it meant nothing as to the fate of the Black Americans, for they still continued to suffer as slaves officially until the declaration of the Emancipation Proclamation on January 1st 1863, and somewhat unofficially till Juneteenth, that is, June 19th, 1866. I say somewhat unofficially because, it ought to be clear to anybody with half a brain by now that, slavery didn't actually end either with Emancipation Proclamation or on Juneteenth, it morphed into racism.

For all these and many more such reasons, recognizing that a people have been wronged doesn't facilitate victim mentality in those people or create division, on the contrary, such an act of admitting error builds real bridges of trust and assimilation. You see, denial of the past doesn't undo the past, it only makes the agony linger longer, especially for those who have been wronged, and therefore it halts the development of a nation.

It is this simple, your intellect may make you feel pompous and superior, but it doesn't necessarily make you human. So, don't - I repeat, don't put too much attention on intellect - intellect is just a tool, that's all, it's not the savior of humanity - the only savior of humanity is common, ordinary, everyday decency. Pure intellect without emotion is like a knife without a handle - does more damage than good. Let me put it another way, someone may be the smartest person on earth, but if they have no humanity in their heart, they are just plain filth.

34. The New StoneAge

There are no angels, only humans acting human. There are no saints, only humans acting human. And the direction in which our society moves is predicated on the actions of these humans. Or to put it another way, if the humans act human, then only the society will move forward towards equality, justice and ascension, or else, it'll continue to move backward and end up creating the modern counterpart of the stoneage - the concrete age, where warmth and acceptance will be an alien concept and indifference and prejudice will be the norm.

Let everyone hear this - we didn't come all this way to replace stone with concrete – we must have heart, we must have dreams, we must have a genuine, invincible desire for universality - otherwise we'll end up with concrete buildings bearing concrete beings.

Substituting stoneage with concrete age is not advancement. Without warmth, logic of concrete is as degrading as the superstition of stone. We are not to be an intellectual species, we are to be a warm species with intellect. Let us be warm, let us be kind, intellect is okay in its place, but it mustn't make us blind.

You see, light can be as blinding as the dark. Hold a flashlight on the street and it brightens your way, but hold it smack right into your eyes and you see nothing - the same is with intellect - too much intellect takes away your humanity. If a person doesn't know how to use a flashlight, it's not the fault of the flashlight, it's the fault of the person holding it. Likewise, to have intellect ain't enough, you must learn how to use it. And you'll know how to use it, when you have a sense of accountability towards your society, and when you have warmth, accountability appears on its own.

Submit to warmth, not intellect, for when you submit to warmth, you conquer the world. Submit to warmth and in this world full of vegetables who submit to prejudice and sectarianism, you'll rise as the conqueror of hearts - and when you've conquered hearts, what good are some puny lands! So, let us be determined, dedicated and indivisible for our conviction of humanity, and rid our hearts of the primeval curse of self-obsession, so that we may turn this dirtland into heartland.

BIBLIOGRAPHY

Archer M., (2000), Being Human: The Problem of Agency. Cambridge University Press.

Archer M., (2003), Structure, Agency and the Internal Conversation. Cambridge University Press.

Adolphs R (2003) Cognitive neuroscience of human social behaviour. Nature Rev Neurosci 4: 165–178.

Adolphs R, Tranel D, Damasio AR (2003) Dissociable neural systems for recognizing emotions. Brain Cogn 52: 61–69.

Afton, A. D. (1985). Forced copulation as a reproductive strategy of male lesser scaup: A field test of some predictions. - Behaviour 92, p. 146-167.

Allison T, Puce A, McCarthy G. (2000) Social perception from visual cues: role of the STS region. Trends Cogn Sci 4: 267–278.

Andresen, Jensine, and Robert Forman, eds. Cognitive Models and Spiritual Maps. Bowling Green, Ohio: Imprint Academic, 2000.

Ashbrook, James, and Carol Albright. The Humanizing Brain: Where Religion and Neuroscience Meet. Cleveland, OH: Pilgrim Press, 1997.

Azari, Nina, Janpeter Nickel, Gilbert Wunderlich, Michael Niedeggen, Harald Hefter, Lutz Tellmann, Hans Herzog, Petra Stoerig, Dieter Birnbacher, and Rudiger Seitz. "Neural Correlates of Religious Experience." European Journal of Neuroscience 13, no. 8 (2001)

Agar, N. (2004). Liberal eugenics: In defence of human enhancement. London: Blackwell Publishing.

Alteheld, N., Roessler, G., Vobig, M., & Walter, R. (2004). The retina implant new approach to a visual prosthesis. Biomedizinische Technik, 49(4), 99–103.

Antal, A., Nitsche, M. A., Kincses, T. Z., Kruse, W., Hoffmann, K. P., & Paulus, W. (2004a). Facilitation of visuo-motor learning by transcranial direct current stimulation of the motor and extrastriate visual areas in humans. European Journal of Neuroscience, 19(10), 2888–2892.

Bernstein R.J., (1971), Praxis and Action: Contemporary Philosophies of Human Activity. Philadelphia: University of Pennsylvania Press.

Bernstein R.J., (1976), The Restructuring Social and Political Thought.

Bernstein R.J., (1983), Beyond Relativism and Objectivism: Science, Hermeneutics, and Praxis. Philadelphia: University of Pennsylvania Press.

Bernstein R.J., (1986), Philosophical Profiles. Philadelphia: University of Pennsylvania Press.

Bernstein R.J., (1991), New Constellation. Cambridge: MIT Press.

Birkhead, T. R., Johnson, S. D. & Nettleship, D. N. (1985). Extra-pair matings and mate guarding in the common murre Uria aalge. - Anim. Behav. 33, p. 608-619.

Beauregard, Mario, and Vincent Paquette. "Neural Correlates of a Mystical Experience in Carmelite Nuns." Neuroscience Letters 405, no. 3 (2006)

Benson, Herbert. Timeless Healing: The Power and Biology of Belief. New York: Scribner, 1996

Bose, Subhas Chandra. An Indian Pilgrim: An Unfinished Autobiography, Oxford University Press, 1997

Bose, Subhas Chandra. The Indian Struggle 1920-1942, Oxford University Press, 1997

Bogen, J.E.(1995a), 'On the neurophysiology of consciousness: Part I. An overview', Consciousness and Cognition, 4.

Bogen, J.E. (1995b), 'On the neurophysiology of consciousness: Part II. Constraining the semantic problem', Consciousness and Cognition, 4.

Bremner, J. D., R. Soufer, et al. (2001). "Gender differences in cognitive and neural correlates of remembrance of emotional words." Psychopharmacol Bull 35 (3).

Brothers, L. (2002). The social brain: A project for integrating primate behavior and neurophysiology in a new domain. In J. T. Cacioppo et al. (Eds.), Foundations in neuroscience. Cambridge, MA: MIT Press.

Buss, D. D. (2003). Evolutionary Psychology: The New Science of Mind, 2nd ed. New York: Allyn & Bacon.

Buss, D. M. (1989). "Conflict between the sexes: Strategic interference and the evocation of anger and upset." J Pers Soc Psychol 56 (5).

Buss, D. M. (1995). "Psychological sex differences. Origins through sexual selection." Am Psychol 50 (3).

Buss, D. M. (2002). "Review: Human Mate Guarding." Neuro Endocrinol Lett 23 (Suppl 4).

Buss, D. M., and D. P. Schmitt (1993). "Sexual strategies theory: An evolutionary perspective on human mating." Psychol Rev 100 (2).

Blakemore SJ, Decety J (2001) From the perception of action to the understanding of intention. Nature Rev Neurosci 2: 561.

Bruce C, Desimone R, Gross CG (1981) Visual properties of neurons in a polysensory area in superior temporal sulcus of the macaque. J Neurophysiol 46: 369–384.

Buccino G, Vogt S, Ritzl A, Fink GR, Zilles K, Freund HJ, Rizzolatti G (2004) Neural circuits underlying imitation of hand actions: an event related fMRI study. Neuron 42: 323–34.

Colapietro V., (1988), "Human Agency: The Habits of Our Being." Southern Journal of Philosophy, XXVI, 2, pp. 153-68.

Colapietro V., (1992), "Purpose, Power, and Agency." The Monist, 75, 4 (October) pp. 423-44.

Colapietro V., (2004a), "C. S. Peirce's Reclamation of Teleology." Nature in American Philosophy, ed. Jean De Groot (Washington, D.C.: Catholic University Press of America), pp. 88-108.

Colapietro V., (2004b), "Portrait of a Historicist: An Alternative Reading of Peircean Semiotic." Semiotiche, 2/04 [maggio 2004], pp. 49-68.

Colapietro V., (2006), "Engaged Pluralism: Between Alterity and Sociality." The Pragmatic Century: Conversations with Richard J. Bernstein (Albany, NY: SUNY Press), pp. 39-68.

Carey DP, Perrett DI, Oram MW (1997) Recognizing, understanding and reproducing actions. In: Jeannerod M, Grafman J (eds) Handbook of neuropsychology. Vol. 11: Action and cognition. Elsevier, Amsterdam.

Carr L, Iacoboni M, Dubeau MC, Mazziotta JC, Lenzi GL (2003) Neural mechanisms of empathy in humans: a relay from neural systems for imitation to limbic areas. Proc Natl Acad Sci USA 100: 5497–5502.

Changeux JP, Ricoeur P (1998) La nature et la règle. Odile Jacob, Paris.

Chomsky Noam, (2017) Requiem for the American Dream

Chomsky Noam, (2016) Who Rules the World?

Chomsky Noam, (2010) How the World Works

Churchland, P.S. (1986), Neurophilosophy (Cambridge, MA: The MIT Press).

Churchland, P.S. & Ramachandran, V.S. (1993), 'Filling in: Why Dennett is wrong', in Dennett and His Critics: Demystifying Mind, ed. B. Dahlbom (Oxford: Blackwell Scientific Press).

Churchland, P.S., Ramachandran, V.S. & Sejnowski, T.J. (1994), 'A critique of pure vision', in Large- scale Neuronal Theories of the Brain, ed. C. Koch & J.L. Davis (Cambridge, MA: The MIT Press).

Coyle EF. Integration of the physiological factors determining endurance performance ability. Exerc Sport Sci Rev. 1995;23:25–63.

Crick, F. (1994), The Astonishing Hypothesis: The Scientific Search for the Soul (New York: Simon and Schuster).

Crick, F. (1996), 'Visual perception: rivalry and consciousness', Nature, 379.

Crick, F. & Koch, C. (1992), 'The problem of consciousness', Scientific American, 267.

Craig AD (2002) How do you feel? Interoception: the sense of the physiological condition of the body. Nature Rev Neurosci 3: 655–666.

Damasio, A (2003a) Looking for Spinoza. Harcourt Inc. Damasio A (2003b) Feeling of emotion and the self. Ann NY Acad Sci 1001: 253–261.

d'Aquili, Eugene. "Senses of Reality in Science and Religion." Zygon 17, no 4 (1982)

d'Aquili, Eugene. "The Biopsychological Determinants of Religious Ritual Behavior." Zygon 10, no. 1 (1975)

d'Aquili, Eugene. "The Myth-Ritual Complex: A Biogenetic Structural Analysis." Zygon 18, no. 3 (1983)

d'Aquili, Eugene, and Andrew Newberg. The Mystical Mind: Probing the Biology of Religious Experience. Minneapolis: Fortress Press, 1999.

Daly DD. 1958. Ictal affect. Am J Psychiatry.

Damasio, A. (1994) Descartes' Error: Emotion, Reason and the Human Brain. New York, Putnams.

Damasio, A. (1999) The Feeling of What Happens: Body, Emotion and the Making of Consciousness. London, Heinemann.

Darwin, C. (1859) On the Origin of Species by Means of Natural Selection. London, Murray.

Darwin, C. (1871) The Descent of Man and Selection in Relation to Sex. London, John Murray.

Darwin, C. (1872) The Expression of the Emotions in Man and Animals. London, John Murray; also published 1965, Chicago, University of Chicago Press.

Dawkins, M.S. (1987) Minding and mattering. In C. Blakemore and S. Greenfield (eds) Mindwaves. Oxford, Blackwell, 151-60.

Dawkins, R. (1976) The Selfish Gene. Oxford, Oxford University Press; a new edition, with additional material, was published in 1989.

Dawkins, R. (1986) The Blind Watchmaker. London, Longman.

Di Pellegrino G, Fadiga L, Fogassi L, Gallese V, Rizzolatti G (1992) Understanding motor events: A neurophysiological study. Exp Brain Res 91: 176–80.

Deikman, A.J. (2000) A functional approach to mysticism. Journal of Consciousness Studies 7(11-12), 75-91.

Delmonte, M.M. (1987) Personality and meditation. In M. West (ed.) The Psychology of Meditation. Oxford, Clarendon Press, 118-32.

Dennett, D.C. (1988) Quining qualia. In A.J. Marcel and E. Bisiach (eds) Consciousness in Contemporary Science. Oxford, Oxford University Press, 42-77.

Dennett, D.C. (1991) Consciousness Explained. Boston, MA, and London, Little, Brown and Co.

Dennett, D.C. (1995a) Darwin's Dangerous Idea. London, Penguin.

Dennett, D.C. (1995b) The unimagined preposterousness of zombies. Journal of Consciousness Studies 2(4), 322-6.

Dennett, D.C. (1995c) Cog: steps towards consciousness in robots. In T. Metzinger (ed.) Conscious Experience. Thorverton, Devon, Imprint Academic, 471-87.

Dennett, D.C. (1996a) Facing backwards on the problem of consciousness. Journal of Consciousness Studies 3(1), 4-6.

Dennett, D.C. (1996b) Kinds of Minds: Towards an Understanding of Consciousness. London, Weidenfeld & Nicolson.

Dennett, D.C. (1997) An exchange with Daniel Dennett. In J. Searle (ed.) The Mystery of Consciousness. New York, New York Review of Books, 115-19.

Dennett, D.C. (1998) The myth of double transduction. In S.R. Hameroff, A.W. Kaszniak and A. C. Scott (eds) Toward a Science of Consciousness: The Second Tucson Discussions and Debates. Cambridge, MA, MIT Press, 97-107.

Dennett, D.C. (1998b) Brainchildren: Essays on Designing Minds. Cambridge, MA, MIT Press.

Dennett, D.C. (2001) The fantasy of first person science. Debate with D. Chalmers, Northwestern University, Evanston, IL, February 2001.

Dennett, D.C. (2003) Freedom Evolves. New York, Penguin.

Dennett, D.C. and Kinsbourne, M. (1992) Time and the observer: the where and when of consciousness in the brain. Behavioral and Brain Sciences 15, 183-247, including commentaries and authors' responses.

Dewey J., (1911 [1977]), "Epistemological Realism: The Alleged Ubiquity of the Knowledge Relation." Journal of Philosophy, VIII, 20 (September 28, 1911).

Dewhurst, Kenneth, and A. W. Beard. "Sudden Religious Conversions in Temporal Lobe Epilepsy." British Journal of Psychiatry 117 (1970)

Dewhurst K, Beard AW. Sudden religious conversions in temporal lobe epilepsy. 1970 Epilepsy Behav 2003

Devinsky O, Lai G. Spirituality and religion in epilepsy. Epilepsy Behav 2008.

Devinsky, O., Morrell, MJ, Vogt, BA. (1995) 'Contribution of anterior cingulate cortex to behavior', Brain, 118.

Douglas Stone A., Chapter 24, The Indian Comet, in the book Einstein and the Quantum, Princeton University Press, Princeton, New Jersey, 2013.

E. Horvitz, "One Hundred Year Study on Artificial Intelligence: Reflections and Framing," ed: Stanford University, 2014.

Einstein A. (1925). "Quantentheorie des einatomigen idealen Gases". Sitzungsberichte der Preussischen Akademie der Wissenschaften.

Eckhart Meister, Selected Writings

Egidi R., ed. (1999), "Von Wright and 'Dante's Dream': Stages in a Philosophical Pilgrim's Progress", in In Search of a New Humanism: the Philosophy of G.H. von Wright, ed. by R. Egidi, Kluwer, Dordrecht.

Fadiga L, Fogassi L, Pavesi G, Rizzolatti G (1995) Motor facilitation during action observation: a magnetic stimulation study. J Neurophysiol 73: 2608–2611.

Fogassi L, Gallese V, Fadiga L, Rizzolatti G (1998) Neurons responding to the sight of goal directed hand/arm actions in the parietal area PF (7b) of the macaque monkey. Soc Neurosci Abs 24:257.5.

Frith U, Frith CD (2003) Development and neurophysiology of mentalizing. Philos Trans R Soc Lond B Biol Sci 358: 459.

Farah, M.J. (1989), 'The neural basis of mental imagery', Trends in Neurosciences, 10.

Finlay BL, Darlington RB (1995) Linked regularities in the development and evolution of mammalian brains. Science 268.

Freud, S. "The Interpretation of Dreams", 1900

Freud, S. "Selected papers on hysteria and other psychoneuroses" Journal of Nervous and Mental Disease 1909.

Freud, S. "The Origin and Development of Psychoanalysis", 1910

Freud, S. "Psychopathology of everyday life", 1914

Freud, S. "Beyond the Pleasure Principle", 1920

Frith, C.D. & Dolan, R.J. (1997), 'Abnormal beliefs: Delusions and memory', Paper presented at the May, 1997, Harvard Conference on Memory and Belief.

Gay, Volney, ed. Neuroscience and Religion. Plymouth, UK: Lexington Books, 2009.

Gazzaniga, M. S. (1985). The social brain. New York: Basic Books.

Gazzaniga, M.S. (1993), 'Brain mechanisms and conscious experience', Ciba Foundation Symposium, 174.

Geschwind N. "Behavioural changes in temporal lobe epilepsy". Psychol Med. 1979.

Gellhorn, E., Kiely, W.F. "Mystical states of consciousness: neurophysiological and clinical aspects." J Nerv Ment Dis. 1972;154:399-405.

Gilbert SL, Dobyns WB, Lahn BT (2005) Genetic links between brain development and brain evolution. Nat Rev Genet 6.

Gray JA. The Psychology of Fear and Stress. 2nd ed. New York, NY: Cambridge University Press; 1988.

Gloor, P. (1992), 'Amygdala and temporal lobe epilepsy', in The Amygdala: Neurobiological Aspects of Emotion, Memory and Mental Dysfunction, ed J.P. Aggleton (New York: Wiley-Liss).

Greenspan, S. I. and S. G. Shanker (2004). The first idea: How symbols, language, and intelligence evolved from our early primate ancestors to modern humans. Cambridge, MA: Da Capo Press.

Grady, D. (1993), 'The vision thing: Mainly in the brain', Discover, June.

Gallagher HL, Frith CD (2003) Functional imaging of 'theory of mind'. Trends Cogn Sci 7: 77.

Gallese V, Fogassi L, Fadiga L, Rizzolatti G (2002) Action representation and the inferior parietal lobule. In: Prinz W, Hommel B (eds) Attention & Performance XIX. Common mechanisms in perception and action. Oxford University Press, Oxford.

Gallese V, Keysers C, Rizzolatti G (2004) A unifying view of the basis of social cognition. Trends Cogn Sci 8: 396–403.

Gangitano M, Mottaghy FM, Pascual-Leone A (2001) Phase specific modulation of cortical motor output during movement observation. NeuroReport 12: 1489–1492.

Gangitano M, Mottaghy FM, Pascual-Leone A (2004) Modulation of premotor mirror neuron activity during observation of unpredictable grasping movements. Eur J Neurosci 20: 2193– 2202.

Goldman AI, Sripada CS (2004) Simulationist models of face-based emotion recognition. Cognition 94: 193–213.

Grèzes J, Costes N, Decety J (1998) Top-down effect of strategy on the perception of human biological motion: a PET investigation. Cogn Neuropsychol 15: 553–582.

Grèzes J, Armony JL, Rowe J, Passingham RE (2003) Activations related to "mirror" and "canonical" neurones in the human brain: an fMRI study. Neuroimage 18: 928–937.

Gross CG, Rocha-Miranda CE, Bender DB (1972) Visual properties of neurons in the inferotemporal cortex of the macaque. J Neurophysiol 35: 96–111.

Hari R, Forss N, Avikainen S, Kirveskari S, Salenius S, Rizzolatti G (1998) Activation of human primary motor cortex during action observation: a neuromagnetic study. Proc. Natl Acad Sci USA 95: 15061–15065.

Hardy, G. H. (1940). Ramanujan. Cambridge: Cambridge University Press.

Hall, Daniel, Keith Meador, and Harold Koenig. "Measuring Religiousness in Health Research: Review and Critique." Journal of Religion and Health 47, no. 2 (2008)

Harris, Sam, Jonas Kaplan, Ashley Curiel, Susan Bookheimer, Marco Iacoboni, and Mark Cohen. "The Neural Correlates of Religious and

Nonreligious Belief." PLoS One 4, no. 10 (October 1, 2009)

Halgren, E. (1992), 'Emotional neurophysiology of the amygdala within the context of human cognition', in The Amygdala: Neurobiological Aspects of Emotion, Memory and Mental Dysfunction, ed J.P. Aggleton (New York: Wiley-Liss).

Halligan PW, Fink GR, Marshal JC, Vallar G. 2003. Spatial cognition: evidence from visual neglect. Trends Cogn Sci.

Handbook of Emotions, Edited by Michael Lewis, Jeannette M. Haviland-Jones, and Lisa Feldman Barrett, The Guilford Press; 3rd edition (2010).

Hameroff, S.R. and Penrose, R. (1996) Conscious events as orchestrated space-time selections. Journal of Consciousness Studies 3(1), 36-53; also reprinted in J. Shear (ed.) (1997) Explaining Consciousness-The Hard

Problem. Cambridge, MA, MIT Press, 177-95.

Harding, D.E. (1961) On Having no Head: Zen and the Re-Discovery of the Obvious. London, Buddhist Society.

Hardy, A. (1979) The Spiritual Nature of Man: A Study of Contemporary Religious Experience. Oxford, Clarendon Press.

Harre, R. and Gillett, G. (1994) The Discursive Mind. Thousand Oaks, CA, Sage.

Haugeland, J. (ed.) (1997) Mind Design II: Philosophy, Psychology, Artificial Intelligence. Cambridge, MA, MIT Press.

Hauser, M.D. (2000) Wild Minds: What Animals Really Think. New York, Henry Holt and Co.; London, Penguin.

Hebb, D.O. (1949) The Organization of Behavior. New York, Wiley.

Helmholtz, H.L.F. von (1856-67) Treatise on Physiological Optics.

Hess, EH (1975) "The role of pupil size in communication," Scientific American, 233(5), 110–12.

Heyes, C.M. (1998) Theory of mind in nonhuman primates. Behavioral and Brain Sciences 21, 101-48; with commentaries.

Heyes, C.M. and Galef, B.G. (eds) (1996) Social Learning in Animals: The Roots of Culture. San Diego, CA, Academic Press.

Hilgard, E.R. (1986) Divided Consciousness: Multiple Controls in Human Thought and Action. New York, Wiley.

Hilton, E.N., Lundberg, T.R. Transgender Women in the Female Category of Sport: Perspectives on Testosterone Suppression and Performance Advantage. Sports Med 51, 199–214 (2021).

Hitler, Adolf. Mein Kampf, 1925

Hodgson, R. (1891) A case of double consciousness. Proceedings of the Society for Psychical Research 7, 221-58.

Hofstadter, D.R. and Dennett, D.C. (eds) (1981) The Mind's I: Fantasies and Reflections on Self and Soul. London, Penguin.

Holland, J. (ed.) (2001) Ecstasy: The Complete Guide: A Comprehensive Look at the Risks and Benefits of MDMA. Rochester, VT, Park Street Press.

Holmes, D.S. (1987) The influence of meditation versus rest on physiological arousal. In M. West (ed.) The Psychology of Meditation. Oxford, Clarendon Press, 81-103.

Holmstrom, David. 1992, Christian Science Monitor

Holt, J. (1999) Blindsight in debates about qualia. Journal of Consciousness Studies 6(5), 54-71.

Holloway RL (1996) Evolution of the human brain. In: Lock A, Peters CR (eds) Handbook of human symbolic evolution. Oxford University Press, Oxford

Iacoboni M, Woods RP, Brass M, Bekkering H, Mazziotta JC, Rizzolatti G (1999) Cortical mechanisms of human imitation. Science 286: 2526–2528.

Iacoboni M, Koski LM, Brass M, Bekkering H, Woods RP, Dubeau MC, Mazziotta JC, Rizzolatti G (2001) Reafferent copies of imitated actions in the right superior temporal cortex. Proc Natl Acad Sci USA 98: 13995–13999.

Jeannerod M (1988) The neural and behavioural organization of goal-directed movements. Clarendon Press, Oxford.

Johnson-Frey SH, Maloof FR, Newman-Norlund R, Farrer C, Inati S, Grafton ST (2003) Actions or hand-objects interactions? Human inferior frontal cortex and action observation. Neuron 39: 1053–1058.

Jackson, F. (1982) Epiphenomenal qualia. Philosophical Quarterly 32, 127-36.

James, W. (1890) The Principles of Psychology (2 volumes). London, Macmillan.

James, W. (1902) The Varieties of Religious Experience: A Study in Human Nature. New York and London, Longmans, Green and Co.

Jansen, K. (2001) Ketamine: Dreams and Realities. Sarasota, FL, Multidisciplinary Association for Psychedelic Studies.

Jay, M. (ed.) (1999) Artificial Paradises: A Drugs Reader. London, Penguin.

Jaynes, J. (1976) The Origin of Consciousness in the Breakdown of the Bicameral Mind. New York, Houghton Mifflin.

Johnson, M.K. and Raye, C.L. (1981) Reality monitoring. Psychological Review 88, 67-85.

Kadim I, Mahgoub O, Baqir S et al. (2015) Cultured meat from muscle stem cells: a review of challenges and prospects. J Integr Agr 14: 222–233

Kandel, E. R. In Search of Memory: The Emergence of a New Science of Mind, W. W. Norton & Company (2007).

Kandel E. R. Schwartz JH, Jessel TM. Principles of neural sciences. New York; McGraw Hill, 2000.

Kanwisher, N. (2001) Neural events and perceptual awareness. Cognition

79, 89-113; also reprinted inS. Dehaene (ed.) The Cognitive Neuroscience of Consciousness. Cambridge, MA, MIT Press, 89-113.

Karn, K. and Hayhoe, M. (2000) Memory representations guide targeting eye movements in a natural task. Visual Cognition 7, 673-703.

Kennedy, H., & Dehay, C. (1988). Functional implications of the anatomical organization of the callosal projections of visual areas V1 and V2 in the macaque monkey. Behav. Brain Res., 29, 225–236.

Kentridge, R.W. and Heywood, C.A. (1999) The status of blindsight. Journal of Consciousness Studies 6(5), 3-11.

Kihlstrom, J.F. (1996) Perception without awareness of what is perceived, learning without awareness of what is learned. In M. Velmans (ed.) The Science of Consciousness. London, Routledge, 23-46.

Kosslyn, S.M. (1980) Image and Mind. Cambridge, MA, Harvard University Press.

Kosslyn, S.M. (1988) Aspects of a cognitive neuroscience of mental imagery. Science 240, 1621-6.

Kinsbourne, M. (1995), 'The intralaminar thalamic nucleii', Consciousness and Cognition, 4.

Kjaer, Troels, Camilla Bertelsen, Paola Piccini, David Brooks, Jorgen Alving, and Hans Lou. "Increased Dopamine Tone during Meditation- Induced Change of Consciousness." Cognitive Brain Research 13, no. 2 (April 2002)

Kölmel HW. 1985. Complex visual hallucinations in the hemianopic field. J Neurol Neurosurg Psychiatry.

Koenig, Harold. "Research on Religion, Spirituality, and Mental Health: A Review." Canadian Journal of Psychiatry 54, no. 5 (May 2009)

Koenig, Harold, ed. Handbook of Religion and Mental Health. San Diego, CA: Academic Press, 1998

Kraepelin E. Psychiatry: A Textbook for Students and Physicians. New York, NY: Science History Publications; 1990.

Lauglin, Charles, John McManus, and Eugene d'Aquili. Brain, Symbol, and Experience. 2nd ed. New York: Columbia University Press, 1992

Lakoff, G. and M. Johnson (1999). Philosophy in the flesh. Basic Books: New York.

LeDoux, J. E. (1996). The emotional brain. New York: Simon & Schuster.

LeDoux, J.E. (1992), 'Emotion and the amygdala', in The Amygdala: Neurobiological Aspects of Emo- tion, Memory and Mental Dysfunction, ed J.P. Aggleton (New York: Wiley-Liss).

Levin, D.T. and Simons, D.J. (1997) Failure to detect changes to attended objects in motion pictures. Psychonomic Bulletin and Review 4, 501-6.

Levine,J. (1983) Materialism and qualia: the explanatory gap. Pacific Philosophical Quarterly 64, 354-61.

Levine,J. (2001) Purple Haze: The Puzzle of Consciousness. New York, Oxford University Press. Levine, S. (1979) A Gradual Awakening. New York, Doubleday.

Levinson, B.W. (1965) States of awareness during general anaesthesia. British Journal of Anaesthesia 37, 544-6.

Lewicki, P., Czyzewska, M. and Hoffman, H. (1987) Unconscious acquisition of complex procedural knowledge. Journal of Experimental Psychology: Learning, Memory and Cognition 13, 523-30.

Lewicki, P., Hill, T. and Bizot, E. (1988) Acquisition of procedural knowledge about a pattern of stimuli that cannot be articulated. Cognitive Psychology 20, 24-37.

Lewicki, P., Hill, T. and Czyzewska, M. (1992) Nonconscious acquisition of information. American Psychologist 47, 796-801.

Manthey S, Schubotz RI, von Cramon DY (2003). Premotor cortex in observing erroneous action: an fMRI study. Brain Res Cogn Brain Res 15: 296–307.

Mesulam MM, Mufson EJ (1982) Insula of the old world monkey. III: Efferent cortical output and comments on function. J Comp Neurol 212: 38–52.

Naskar, Abhijit. "Homo: A Brief History of Consciousness", 2015

Naskar, Abhijit. "What is Mind?", 2016

Naskar, Abhijit. "Love, God & Neurons: Memoir of A Scientist who found himself by getting lost", 2016

Naskar, Abhijit. "Principia Humanitas", 2017

Naskar, Abhijit. "We Are All Black: A Treatise on Racism", 2017

Naskar, Abhijit. "Either Civilized or Phobic: A Treatise on Homosexuality", 2017

Naskar, Abhijit. "I Am The Thread: My Mission", 2017

Naskar, Abhijit. "The Bengal Tigress: A Treatise on Gender Equality", 2017

Naskar, Abhijit. "Morality Absolute", 2017

Naskar, Abhijit. "Build Bridges not Walls: In the name of Americana", 2018

Naskar, Abhijit. "Fabric of Humanity", 2018

Naskar, Abhijit. "Lives To Serve Before I Sleep", 2019

Naskar, Abhijit. "Citizens of Peace: Beyond the Savagery of Sovereignty", 2019

Naskar, Abhijit. "The Constitution of The United Peoples of Earth", 2019

Naskar, Abhijit. "Neurons Giveth, Neurons Taketh Away | Abhijit Naskar | TEDxIIMRanchi", 2019 https://www.youtube.com/watch?v=BNX-Q0ySm80

Naskar, Abhijit. "Mission Reality", 2019

Naskar, Abhijit. "Operation Justice: To Make A Society That Needs No Law", 2019

Naskar, Abhijit. "Every Generation Needs Caretakers: The Gospel of Patriotism", 2020

Naskar, Abhijit. "Hurricane Humans: Give me accountability, I'll give you peace", 2020

Naskar, Abhijit. "Revolution Indomable", 2020

Naskar, Abhijit. "Servitude is Sanctitude", 2020

Naskar, Abhijit. "Good Scientist: When Science and Service Combine", 2020

Newberg, Andrew, and Jeremy Iversen. "The Neural Basis of the Complex Mental Task of Meditation: Neurotransmitter and Neurochemical Considerations." Medical Hypotheses 61, no. 2 (2003).

Newberg, Andrew. "How God Changes Your Brain: An Introduction to Jewish Neurotheology", CCAR Journal: The Reform Jewish Quarterly, Winter 2016.

Newberg, Andrew, and Stephanie Newberg. "A Neuropsychological

Perspective on Spiritual Development." In Handbook of Spiritual Development in Childhood and Adolescence, edited by Eugene Roehlkepartain, Pamela King, Linda Wagener, and Peter Benson. London: Sage Publications, Inc., 2005

Newberg, Andrew. "The Neurotheology Link An Intersection Between Spirituality and Health", Alternative and Complimentary Therapies, Vol 21 No 1, February 2015.

Newberg, Andrew, Nancy Wintering, Dharma Khalsa, Hannah Roggenkamp, and Mark Waldman. "Meditation Effects on Cognitive Function and Cerebral Blood Flow in Subjects with Memory Loss: A Preliminary Study." Journal of Alzheimer's Disease 20, no. 2 (2010)

Nash, M. (1995), 'Glimpses of the mind', Time.

Nesse RM. Proximate and evolutionary studies of anxiety, stress and depression: synergy at the interface. Neurosci Biobehav Rev. 1999;23:895-903.

Nicolelis, Miguel. (2011) "Beyond Boundaries: The New Neuroscience of Connecting Brains with Machines---and How It Will Change Our Lives", Times Books

O'Hara, K. and Scutt, T. (1996) There is no hard problem of consciousness. Journal of Consciousness Studies 3(4), 290-302, reprinted in J. Shear (ed.) (1997) Explaining Consciousness. Cambridge, MA, MIT Press, 69-82.

O'Regan, J.K. (1992) Solving the "real" mysteries of visual perception: the world as an outside memory. Canadian Journal of Psychology 46, 461-88.

O'Regan, J.K. and Noe, A. (2001) A sensorimotor account of vision and visual consciousness. Behavioral and Brain Sciences 24(5), 883-917.

O'Regan, J.K., Rensink, R.A. and Clark,].]. (1999) Change-blindness as a result of "mudsplashes." Nature 398, 34.

Ornstein, R.E. (1977) The Psychology of Consciousness (2nd edn). New York, Harcourt.

Ornstein, R.E. (1986) The Psychology of Consciousness (3rd edn). New York, Pehguin.

Ornstein, R.E. (1992) The Evolution of Consciousness. New York, Touchstone.

Penfield W, Faulk ME (1955) The insula: further observations on its function. Brain 78: 445– 470.

Penrose, R. (1994), Shadows of the Mind (Oxford: Oxford University Press).

Penrose, R. (1989), The Emperor's New Mind: Concerning Computers, Minds and The Laws of Physics (Oxford: Oxford University Press).

Persinger, "'I would kill in God's name' role of sex, weekly church attendance, report of a religious experience and limbic lability" Perceptual and Motor Skills 1997.

Persinger "Experimental simulation of the God experience" Neurotheology 2003.

Persinger, M. A. (1993b). Personality changes following brain injury as a grief response to the loss of sense of self: Phenomenological themes as indices of local lability and neurocognitive restructuring as psycho- therapy. Psychological Reports, 72

Persinger, Corradini, Clement, Keaney, et al "Neurotheology and its convergence with neuroquantology" NeuroQuantology 2010.

Persinger, Koren and St-Pierre "The electromagnetic induction of mystical and altered states within the laboratory" Journal of Consciousness Exploration and Research 2010.

Persinger "Case report: A prototypical spontaneous 'sensed presence' of a sentient being and concomitant electroencephalographic activity in the clinical laboratory" Neurocase 2008.

Persinger and Saroka "Potential production of Hughlings Jackson's "parasitic consciousness" by physiologically-patterned weak transcerebral magnetic fields: QEEG and source localization" Epilepsy & Behavior 28 (2013).

Persinger. "The neuropsychiatry of paranormal experiences". J Neuropsychiatry Clin Neurosci 2001.

Persinger. "Neuropsychological bases of god beliefs", New York: Praeger, 1987

Persinger. "Temporal lobe epileptic signs and correlative behaviors displayed by normal populations", Journal of General Psychology, 1986

Perry BD, Pollard R. Homeostasis, stress, trauma, and adaptation. A neurodevelopmental view of childhood trauma. Child Adolesc Psychiatr Clin N Am. 1998;7:33.

Paré, D. & Llinás, R. (1995), 'Conscious and preconscious processes as seen from the standpoint of sleep-waking cycle neurophysiology', Neuropsychologia, 33.

Phillips ML, Young AW, Senior C, Brammer M, Andrew C, Calder AJ, Bullmore ET, Perrett DI, Rowland D, Williams SC, Gray JA, David AS (1997) A specific neural substrate for perceiving facial expressions of disgust. Nature 389: 495–498.

Phillips ML, Young AW, Scott SK, Calder AJ, Andrew C, Giampietro V, Williams SC, Bullmore ET, Brammer M, Gray JA (1998) Neural responses to facial and vocal expressions of fear and disgust. Proc R Soc Lond B Biol Sci 265: 1809–1817.

Puce A, Perrett D (2003) Electrophysiological and brain imaging of biological motion. Philosoph Trans Royal Soc Lond, Series B, 358: 435–445.

Ramachandran VS. Behavioral and magnetoencephalographic correlates of plasticity in the adult human brain. Proc Natl Acad Sci USA 1993; 90: 10413–20.

Ramachandran VS. Phantom limbs, neglect syndromes, repressed memories, and Freudian psychology. Int Rev Neurobiol 1994; 37: 291–333.

Ramachandran VS. Plasticity and functional recovery in neurology. Clin Med 2005; 5: 368–73.

Ramachandran VS, Hirstein W. The perception of phantom limbs. The D. O. Hebb lecture. Brain 1998; 121: 1603–30.

Ramachandran VS, Rogers-Ramachandran D, Cobb S. Touching the phantom limb. Nature 1995; 377: 489–90.

Ramachandran VS, Rogers-Ramachandran D. Phantom limbs and neural plasticity. Arch Neurol 2000; 57: 317–20.

Ramachandran VS, Rogers-Ramachandran D. It's all done with mirrors. Sci Am Mind 2007; 18: 16–9.

Ramachandran VS, Rogers-Ramachandran D. Sensations referred to a patient's phantom arm from another subjects intact arm: perceptual correlates of mirror neurons. Med Hypotheses 2008; 70: 1233–4.

Ramachandran VS, Rogers-Ramachandran D, Stewart M. Perceptual correlates of massive cortical reorganization. Science 1992; 258: 1159–60.

Rizzolatti G, Craighero L (2004) The mirror-neuron system. Annu Rev Neurosci 27: 169–192.

Rizzolatti G, Fogassi L, Gallese V (2001) Neurophysiological mechanisms underlying the understanding and imitation of action. Nature Rev Neurosci 2:661–670.

Rock I, Victor J. Vision and touch: an experimentally created conflict between the two senses. Science 1964; 143: 594–6.

Rose'n B, Lundborg G. Training with a mirror in rehabilitation of the hand. Scand J Plast Reconstr Surg Hand Surg 2005; 39: 104–8.

Roberts, TA; Smalley, J; Ahrendt, D (December 2020). "Effect of gender affirming hormones on athletic performance in transwomen and transmen: implications for sporting organisations and legislators". British Journal of Sports Medicine. 55 (11): 577–583

Royet JP, Plailly J, Delon-Martin C, Kareken DA, Segebarth C (2003) fMRI of emotional responses to odors: influence of hedonic valence and judgment, handedness, and gender. Neuroimage 20: 713–728.

Rozin R Haidt J and McCauley CR (2000) Disgust. In: Lewis M, Haviland-Jones JM (eds) Handbook of Emotion. 2nd Edition. Guilford Press, New York, pp 637–653.

Saxe R, Carey S, Kanwisher N (2004) Understanding other minds: linking developmental psychology and functional neuroimaging. Annu Rev Psychol 55: 87–124.

S. J. Russell and P. Norvig, Artificial intelligence: a modern approach (3rd edition): Prentice Hall, 2009.

Singer T, Seymour B, O'Doherty J, Kaube H, Dolan RJ, Frith CD (2004) Empathy for pain involves the affective but not the sensory components of pain. Science 303: 1157–1162.

Smith A (1759) The theory of moral sentiments (ed. 1976). Clarendon Press, Oxford.

Sprengelmeyer R, Rausch M, Eysel UT, Przuntek H (1998) Neural structures associated with recognition of facial expressions of basic emotions Proc R Soc Lond B Biol Sci 265: 1927–1931.

Strafella AP, Paus T (2000) Modulation of cortical excitability during action observation: a transcranial magnetic stimulation study. NeuroReport 11: 2289–2292.

Schilling, Vincent. 2017, indian country today

Stein, Stephen K. 2017, The Sea in World History: Exploration, Travel, and Trade

Simonsen R (2015) Eating for the future: veganism and the challenge of in vitro meat. In: Stapleton P, Byers A (Hg). Biopolitics and utopia. Palgrave Macmillan, New York (2015), S 167–190

Tanaka K (1996) Inferotemporal cortex and object vision. Ann Rev Neurosci. 19: 109–140.

Tesla N. "My Inventions", 1919

T. R. Society, "Machine learning: the power and promise of computers that learn by example," ed. The Royal Society, 2017.

Tomasello M, Call J (1997) Primate cognition. Oxford University Press, Oxford.

Tremblay C, Robert M, Pascual-Leone A, Lepore F, Nguyen DK, Carmant L, Bouthillier A, Theoret H (2004) Action observation and execution: intracranial recordings in a human subject. Neurology. 63: 937–938.

Umilta MA, Kohler E, Gallese V, Fogassi L, Fadiga L, Keysers C, Rizzolatti G (2001) "I know what you are doing": a neurophysiological study. Neuron 32: 91–101.

Wiik, Anna; Lundberg, Tommy R; Rullman, Eric; Andersson, Daniel P; Holmberg, Mats; Mandić, Mirko; Brismar, Torkel B; Dahlqvist Leinhard, Olof; Chanpen, Setareh; Flanagan, John N; Arver, Stefan; Gustafsson, Thomas (1 March 2020). "Muscle Strength, Size, and Composition Following 12 Months of Gender-affirming Treatment in Transgender Individuals". The Journal of Clinical Endocrinology & Metabolism. 105 (3): e805–e813.

www.ingramcontent.com/pod-product-compliance
Lightning Source LLC
Chambersburg PA
CBHW051253250726
48656CB00004B/1265